CW01666558

Bolsover Castle

DERBYSHIRE

P A FAULKNER FSA, ARIBA
Formerly Superintending Architect in charge of Ancient Monuments and Historic Buildings

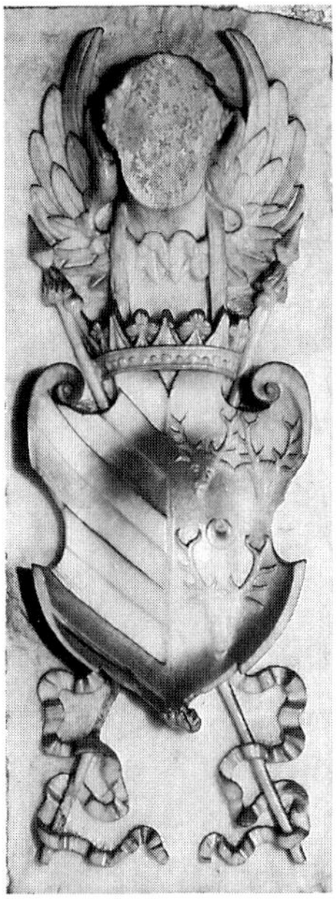

Dominating the landscape, Bolsover Castle rises impressively from a hill top. Castle in name only, the existing early seventeenth-century mansion was built on the site of a twelfth-century castle. Most of it was built for Sir Charles Cavendish and his son William to the designs of Robert, John and Huntingdon Smithson.

The family suite in the self-contained 'keep' is richly decorated with allegorical paintings and carved fireplaces. There is a state range, now roofless, and one of the earliest indoor riding schools.

The Little Castle, separate and self-contained, is a delightful romantic folly decorated in Jacobean style.

This handbook gives a concise history of Bolsover Castle. The description and plans will help to make the history more easily appreciated and a visit to the castle more enjoyable.

The illustration above shows the arms of Cavendish impaling Talbot.

English Heritage
LONDON

CONTENTS

© Crown copyright 1972
Published by HMSO 1972, reprinted 1975
First published by English Heritage 1985, reprinted 1988, 1991, 1992
Printed in England for Her Majesty's Stationery Office
Dd 6041412 C50 8/92 522/1 21954
ISBN 1 85074 048 8

SUMMARY

View from the southwest

There has been a castle at Bolsover since the twelfth century, when William Peverel the second fortified the isolated spur with a CURTAIN WALL (see Glossary) of masonry. To this Henry II added a stone keep about 1173. In the early years of the thirteenth century domestic buildings were added and, shortly afterwards, Peverel's curtain was strengthened by additional towers.

By the end of the fourteenth century the castle had fallen out of use and was almost ruinous. It remained in royal hands for the greater part of the Middle Ages until 1553 when it was granted to Sir George Talbot, sixth Earl of Shrewsbury, husband to 'Bess of Hardwick,' whose son by an earlier marriage, Charles Cavendish, purchased castle and manor from the seventh earl.

Charles Cavendish and his heir, William, later first Duke of Newcastle, between them destroyed the medieval castle and built the mansion, the remains of which now stand on the site. The buildings were started about 1608 and continued with many changes, to the successive designs of Robert, John and Huntingdon Smithson (sometimes spelt Smythson), until 1640. The long Terrace Range to the west of the Great Court was the mansion proper and survived until the mid-eighteenth century.

South of the court the Riding School, forge and stable are entirely the work of William Cavendish, the 'Horsemanship' Duke of Newcastle. To the north is the Little Castle. Though a complete house, it was built as a romantic folly with VAULTED chambers, wall paintings, exuberantly designed fireplaces, and BATTLEMENTED turrets and still contains important early seventeenth-century interior decorations.

The castle was abandoned as a residence in favour of Welbeck by the Dukes of Portland in the early eighteenth century and finally presented as a gift to the nation by the seventh Duke of Portland in 1945.

DESCRIPTION

Outer Court

The gate by which visitors enter Bolsover Castle is at the southeast angle of what was the outer BAILEY (see Glossary) of the medieval castle. The road curving away on their left, past the modern school buildings, to the southwest gate (not open to the public) represents the southern limit of the bailey and may be the site of the ditch which would probably have cut off the promontory on which the castle stands from the town to the south.

No medieval walls survive enclosing the bailey nor has any evidence survived to show that they existed; the steep slopes to the east and west may have been considered adequate defences in themselves.

The seventeenth-century Cavendish buildings cut the former outer bailey into two, a northern Great Court and a southern Outer Court, known then as Castle Yard, an area now occupied by the drive to the southeast gate, the school playing fields, the Bolsover bowling green and the school buildings.

No trace remains of the stables, barns, lodgings, brewhouses and other such buildings which were needed to service the Cavendish mansion and which were disposed around Castle Yard. It is probable that these were the buildings pulled down for the sake of the materials they contained after the castle had been sold by Parliament in 1649–50. The demolition was stopped when Sir William's brother, Sir Charles Cavendish, repurchased the castle and some portion of the stables, at least, survived to need repairs when the buildings were rehabilitated in 1666.

On the southern side of the outer court is a range of buildings, now only partly roofed, which extends from the southwest to the southeast gate. First, at the western end, is the asymmetrical southern end of the Terrace Range of 1635–40, on the left a large arched window with ARCHITRAVE and KEYSTONE which marks the end of the gallery and, to the right, the windows of the state bedchamber, replicas of the contemporary windows facing the Great Court. The PARAPET is straight, punctuated by DIES with sunk FIELDED PANELS.

Eastward a short bay, contemporary with the south end of the Terrace Range, with a similar parapet and containing the upper and lower windows of the vestibule to the private apartments, adjoins Huntingdon Smithson's Riding School Range of 1630–34. It is roofed for its whole length with a pitched roof running down on to moulded eaves brackets.

First is a two-storey section, the private apartments, the dormer missing but surviving windows with architraves and CORNICE HOODS; then a doorway, blocked, with plain sunk classic architrave. Beyond are the four large windows of the forge, this time without hoods, with three dormers spaced above similar in detail to those facing the Great Court.

Next, set forward with the angles marked by projecting QUOINS, is the Riding School. Its five windows have architrave surrounds with cornice hoods over a PULVINATED FRIEZE and, above them, three stone dormers cut into the roof line. Last is the eastern block. Here there are no dormers. On the first floor the windows of the viewing gallery and ante-room have architraves, pulvinated frieze and cornice hoods (some are modern replacements). At half-level is the stair window and, on the ground floor, that of the harness room, both of which originally matched the first-

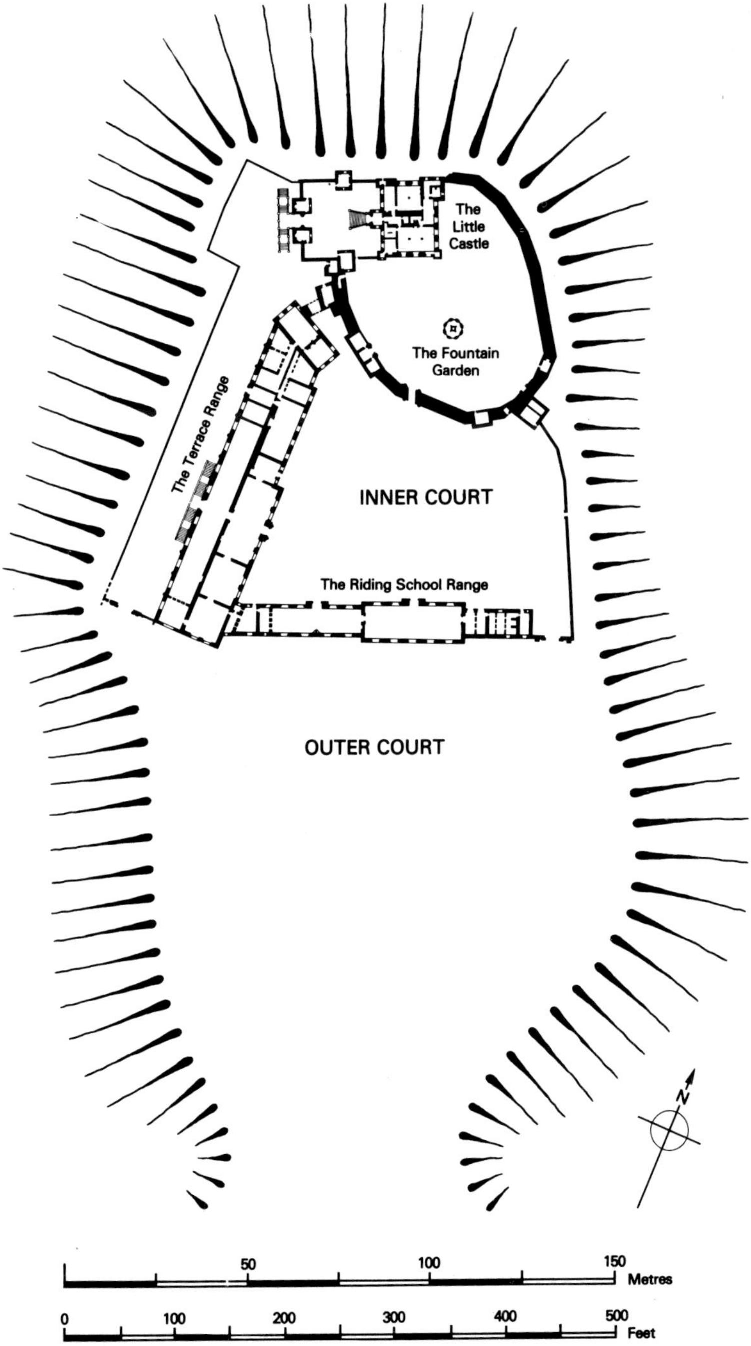
The Little Castle
The Fountain Garden
The Terrace Range
INNER COURT
The Riding School Range
OUTER COURT
N
0
50
100
150
Metres
100
200
300
400
500
Feet

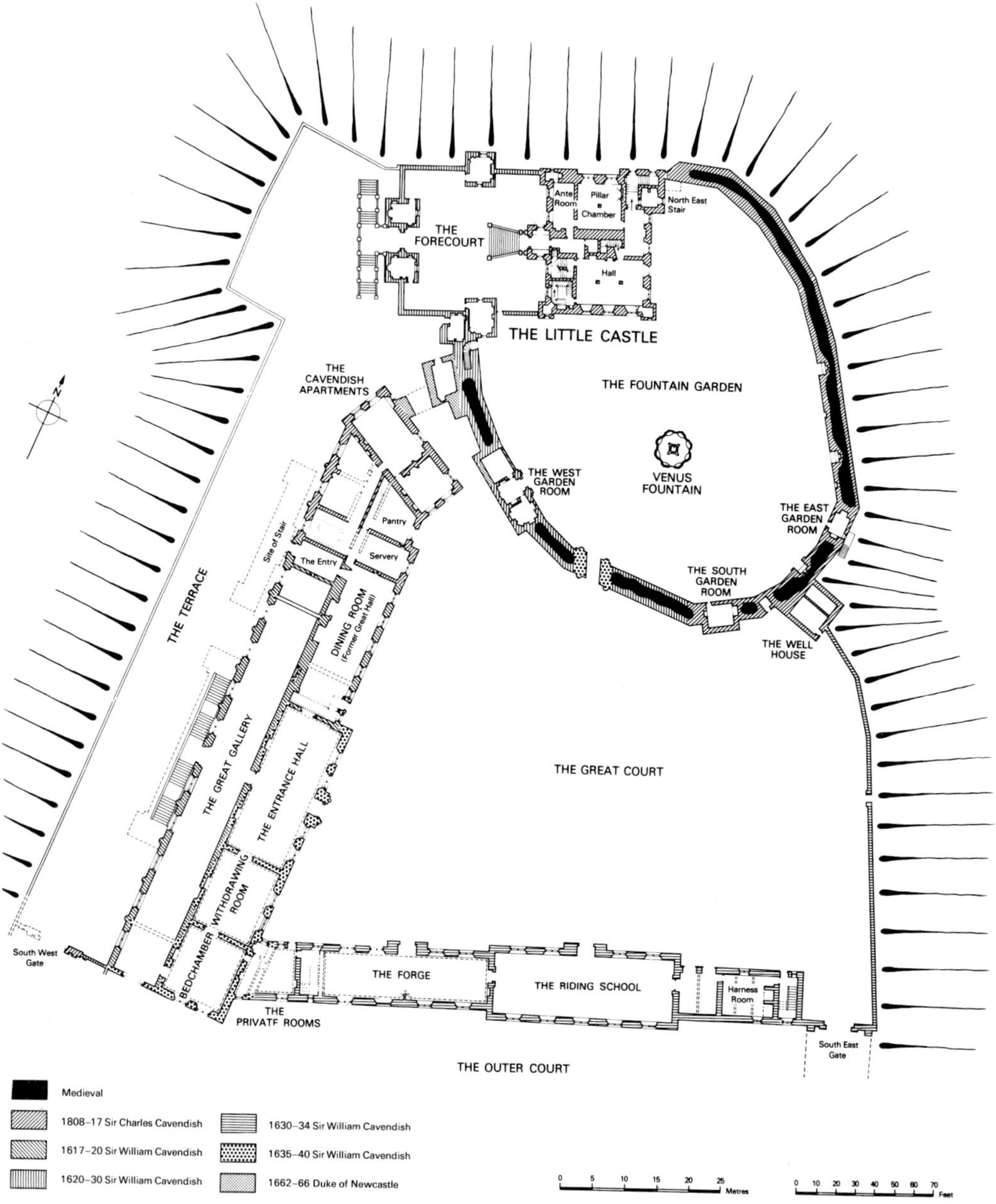
THE FORECOURT
Ante Room
Pillar Chamber
North East Stair
Hall
THE LITTLE CASTLE
THE CAVENDISH APARTMENTS
THE FOUNTAIN GARDEN
VENUS FOUNTAIN
THE WEST GARDEN ROOM
THE EAST GARDEN ROOM
THE SOUTH GARDEN ROOM
THE WELL HOUSE
Pantry
Servery
The Entry
Site of Stair
DINING ROOM (Former Great Hall)
THE TERRACE
THE GREAT GALLERY
THE ENTRANCE HALL
WITHDRAWING ROOM
BEDCHAMBER
THE GREAT COURT
South West Gate
THE PRIVATE ROOMS
THE FORGE
THE RIDING SCHOOL
Harness Room
South East Gate
THE OUTER COURT
Medieval
1808–17 Sir Charles Cavendish
1617–20 Sir William Cavendish
1620–30 Sir William Cavendish
1630–34 Sir William Cavendish
1635–40 Sir William Cavendish
1662–66 Duke of Newcastle
0 5 10 15 20 25 Metres
0 10 20 30 40 50 60 70 Feet

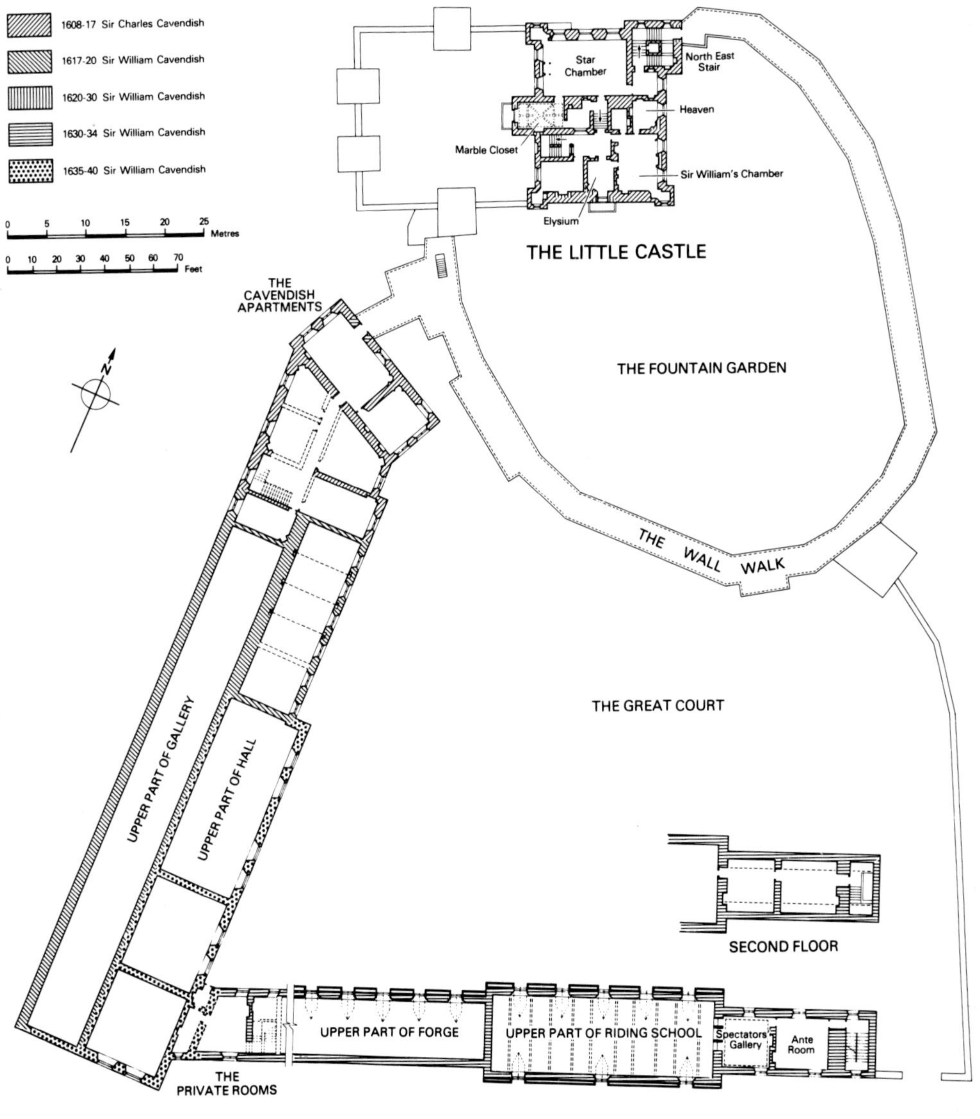

1608-17 Sir Charles Cavendish
1617-20 Sir William Cavendish
1620-30 Sir William Cavendish
1630-34 Sir William Cavendish
1635-40 Sir William Cavendish
0 5 10 15 20 25 Metres
0 10 20 30 40 50 60 70 Feet
N
Star Chamber
North East Stair
Heaven
Marble Closet
Sir William's Chamber
Elysium
THE LITTLE CASTLE
THE CAVENDISH APARTMENTS
THE FOUNTAIN GARDEN
THE WALL WALK
THE GREAT COURT
UPPER PART OF GALLERY
UPPER PART OF HALL
SECOND FLOOR
UPPER PART OF FORGE
UPPER PART OF RIDING SCHOOL
Spectators' Gallery
Ante Room
THE PRIVATE ROOMS

floor windows but the latter had been converted to a door and again reconverted into a window.

At the extreme east end of the range is the southeast gate, the entrance to the Great Court. Modern gates are hung to square RUSTICATED gate piers surmounted by stone balls; flanking these are higher attached rusticated Doric columns carrying ENTABLATURE and BALL FINIALS.

Great Court

The northern half of the medieval outer bailey now forms the Great Court of the Cavendish house. Nearest, when entering by the southeast gate, is the Riding School Range forming the south side of the court; on the west is the roofless Terrace Range; on the north the wall of the Fountain Garden, representing the CURTAIN WALL of the medieval inner bailey; and a boundary wall on the east that crowns the natural escarpment above the lower town of Bolsover.

Riding School Range

Except for the width of the southeast gate, the tripartite Riding School Range occupies the whole of the south side of the court, dominated, as its name implies, by the Riding School itself, the middle though not the largest of the three blocks. Apart from a diminutive bay at the west end it is a unified design by Huntingdon Smithson of 1630–34 built for Sir William Cavendish, by then Viscount Mansfield.

The whole range is a single conception with the symmetrical façade of the Riding School standing slightly forward. This is five bays wide, in coursed ashlar with raised QUOINS at the angles and a central doorcase feature designed as a rusticated triumphal gateway surmounted by a broken segmental pediment with a heavy ball finial at its centre. The four windows have hoods which repeat the entablature of the doorcase. They were initially designed to be lower and to line with those to the west but, perhaps in execution, were later raised.

Above each window and over the door are stone dormers with two-light windows, the OGEE gables of which have copings that terminate in tight scrolls with fishtail ends over the cornice and support alternate segmental and triangular pediments. This form of gable had first appeared in England only fifteen years before in the houses of Sir Fulk Greville and Lady Cooke in Holborn, both recorded by John Smithson on his London visit in 1618–19. The tiled roof runs down to deep eaves between the dormers where each rafter is supported on a stone console bracket. The Riding School roof, being higher than the adjoining roofs, runs into gable ends topped by squat stacks.

The eastern block is the smallest of the three that make up the range. Three-storeyed, it is symmetrical above the ground floor, three bays wide with dormers and two-light first-floor windows which continue both the detail and rhythm of the Riding School. On the ground floor are the door and window to the staircase under a common head with a contemporary oak door, then the two-light harness room window and, lastly, a pair of wide stable doors with quoins, straight arches and dividing pier all rusticated, each originally hung with double doors.

It was first intended to close the court by continuing this building, or a screen wall on its line, to the eastern boundary. In the event this was abandoned for the existing southeast gate, leaving only the quoins for an opening and the toothing of the wall above.

Westward is the forge, repeating the composition of the Riding School but with slightly narrower bays, its windows in the unaltered lower position and with plainer rustications to the otherwise similar centre feature. Of its five bays the last two are roofless. The western limit of the forge is marked only by a change in the FENESTRATION, which here reverts to the rhythm of the eastern block for two bays, the second with a coupled door and window on the ground floor as at the extreme eastern end of the range.

This door formed the private entrance to the Earl of Newcastle's personal suite of rooms, now roofless and in ruins. These filled the space between the forge and the Terrace Range, to which they are joined by a single canted bay that marks the junction between the work of Huntingdon Smithson and his successor who carried out the works of 1635–40.

Terrace Range

The whole of the western side of the court is taken up by the Terrace Range which represents the mansion proper. An irregular whole, it owes its appearance to the staccato manner in which it was built to meet the succeeding changes in design and taste over the thirty years or so which separate the start of the work by Sir Charles Cavendish at the north end from its completion about 1640 by his son, then Earl of Newcastle, at the south.

The dominant feature is the southern block containing the earl's state rooms, which is set forward and clearly differentiated from the gabled remainder by it striking fenestration and CRENELLATED parapet. This portion was erected in 1635–40 by an unknown designer whose strongly individual style contrasts with the work of Huntingdon Smithson on the adjoining Riding School.

The windows of the entrance hall, in pairs flanking the doorway, are treated externally as a two-storeyed composition with cross-windows in the lower stage and squat, undivided, windows above. The upper openings are set within a continuous architrave which is, in turn, surrounded by a picture-frame of heavy SCROLLWORK filling the entire space between the cornice and the lower windows. These have an architrave surround and an entablature and sill which, in each case, breaks forward over side consoles with panels between them.

Well spaced to the south, the windows of the withdrawing room are similarly treated as a group.

Above a narrow cornice, the parapet is interrupted by CORBELLED dies with fielded panels spaced in pairs to reflect the window composition below and continuing the theme of John Smithson's earlier parapet to the Terrace façade. The northeast angle of the building is treated with projecting quoins and there is a square PLINTH.

The strongly sculptural main doorcase is a refinement of those in the Riding School Range. The composition is again rusticated and set forward from the main face with a square-headed opening flanked by COMPOSITE columns standing before pilasters which are concave to receive them. The rustications are not taken across the columns, which are plain apart from a decorated band at about one-third height. The segmental pediment above has raised panels in the frieze and, in the centre, a large achievement of the arms of Newcastle, quarterly 1 Cavendish, 2 Hardwick, 3 Ogle, 4 Bertram, surrounded by the Garter with Cavendish stage supporters, all placed here to mark his rehabilitation of the buildings after the Civil War.

To the north of the new state rooms the range is the work of the two Smithsons, Robert and his son, John. Its most marked characteristic is the line of ogee-pedimented gables. The first five are to one design, clearly the fruit of John Smithson's visit to London and improved upon by Huntingdon Smithson in the dormer gables of the Riding School. The northernmost, with its quadrant curves, is the more 'Jacobean' in treatment and is the only one completed by Robert Smithson when the range was left partially

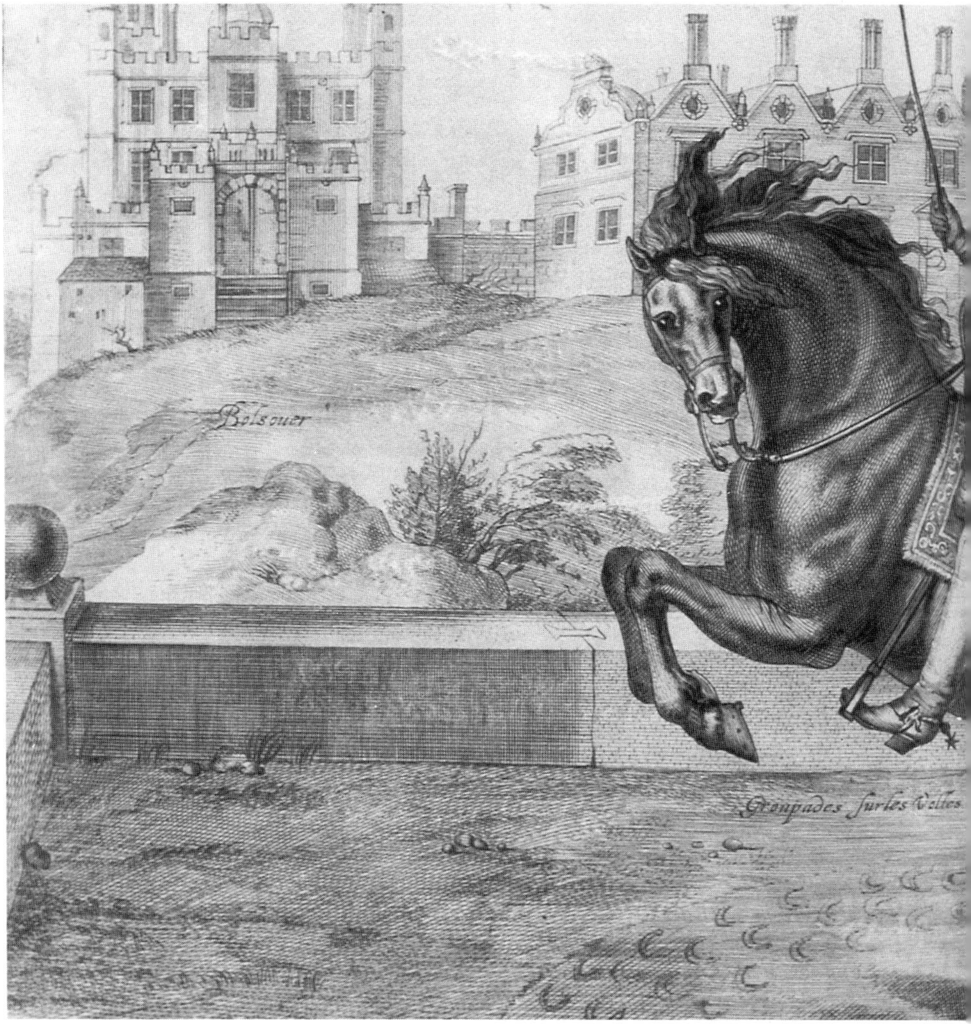

Engraving from the Earl of Newcastle's 'La Méthode et Invention Nouvelle de Dresser les Chevaux', showing Bolsover Castle in the background. Published 1658, but the engraving is probably based on a sketch of c1620

completed at the death of Sir Charles Cavendish in 1617. At this time the northern block had been completed, the next two bays finished up to the heads of the first-floor windows and the whole of the basement built.

On the Terrace façade the gables had been completed. They had straight copings with tall stacks at the apex and carried a circular eye window similar to those surviving in the north bay. The details of the two builds vary little; windows are square-headed with ogee- and FILLET-moulded MULLION and TRANSOM,

Courtauld Institute and British Museum

with a square label mould above and a STRING COURSE between the storeys. When work was resumed in 1619 the detail treatment was continued with a slight variation in the quoins to the windows, the later work showing smaller and more frequent bonding stones.

The remaining three bays up to the new state rooms represent John Smithson's revised design of 1619. These include the four tall three-light windows to his great hall and, under the southern gable, the windows to the great stair that was to serve the projected two-storeyed range on the site of the state rooms. When this stair was altered in 1635–40 the entrance door and the small window to the south were taken out and reset in reverse order.

North wall

The northern boundary of the Great Court is formed by part of the wall of the Fountain Garden. Opposite the northern end of the Terrace Range is the projection formed by the west garden room, perhaps the site of the medieval gatehouse to the inner bailey.

East of this is the present gateway, inserted into the wall by Huntingdon Smithson to lie on the axis of his Riding School and the Little Castle in 1630–35. It is a semicircular-headed gateway set in a surround with heavily rusticated bands which embrace two flanking IONIC columns. There is no entablature but in each case a stone pineapple is placed on a die of the otherwise missing BALUSTRADE of the wall walk.

East again is the projection formed by the rear wall of the south garden room and, beyond that, at the point at which the curtain wall turns north is the well house. In the Buck brothers' engraving of the castle made in 1727 this is shown with a crenellated parapet, one die of which remains at the southeast angle, and surmounted by a CUPOLA which has since been removed. Its interior has been altered but originally contained the spring-fed well and a cistern supplied by a lead pipe from the surviving conduit house on the opposite side of the valley.

The erection of the well house was one of the first operations undertaken by Sir Charles Cavendish in 1612 and is referred to in the accounts for February of that year as 'the spring against the castle,' work on which necessitated 'taking down one piece of the great wall,' that is, the 11ft (3.4m) thick medieval inner curtain. It was natural that the provision of a water supply for his new building work should be Sir Charles's first concern, to be carried out, as the accounts show, at the same time as the masons' lodges were erected and the lime kilns built.

Southwards from the well house the Great Court is closed by a boundary wall with a rusticated doorway at its centre. It is contemporary with the southeast gate to which it is joined, being part of the work completed in 1634 to tidy up the court before the royal entertainment of that year.

Riding School Range: interior

Riding School

Inspection of the interior of the Riding School Range must inevitably start with the Riding School itself. It was designed by Huntingdon Smithson for indoor equestrian exercise and the display of high school riding or *manège*. Nowadays the Riding for the Disabled organisation makes use of it, and its interior may normally be viewed only from the gallery of the Riding Master's lodging in the east block. Measuring some 92 by 30ft (28 by 9m) internally, it is slightly smaller than the similar building erected by Smithson for Sir William at Welbeck in 1625. The original double doors still hang in the doorway, elaborately panelled in diamond, square and other geometric shapes. In the door on the left is a wicket.

The fenestration is symmetrical, five large windows on the south side and four – two on either side of the doorway – on the north. There has been an alteration in the design of these windows, which were originally to be lower to line with those of the forge to the west, with sloping, later converted to square, internal sills. Above the main windows additional light is given by dormers, five above the windows and door on the north and three on the south.

The walls were finished in plain plaster, of which considerable areas remain. In the

Interior of the Riding School (photograph taken during repairs)

east and west walls are door surrounds with straight arches over the openings and characteristically heavy block rustication to their jambs and heads. The doors are set to the north of the centre line and over the eastern are the three openings to the gallery, from which the company could view the demonstrations of horsemanship below.

A cornice broken by keystones runs across the side openings which are flanked by a pilaster motif carried round the centre opening as an architrave, in turn interrupted by an ogee keystone. A similar cornice supported on four BAROQUE consoles serves as a sill. A small cupboard recess is set in the east wall to the north of the doorcase. Above tie-beam level the ends have, in addition, square-headed openings with ashlar surrounds. Their purpose is obscure as there does not appear to have been a floor at this level originally, though one existed in later days.

The Riding School retains its original open roof. Unlike the design for the hammer-beam roof over the Welbeck riding school this is supported on ten tie-beam TRUSSES with wall trusses at either end. The ties have quadrant braces beneath them which are housed into wall posts resting on stone corbels. Above the tie-beam two QUEEN POSTS support a mid-height collar to which they are braced with near-quadrant braces. A KING POST rises from the centre of the collar to the apex of the truss, an openwork pendant being mounted on the underside of the collar immediately beneath it. Both tie-beams and collars are braced to the truss PRINCIPALS with curved braces.

Common rafters are supported on three sets of PURLINS housed into the principals to which they are straight braced, above and below, at each end. The lower purlins are omitted in those bays which contain dormers. The underside of the tie-beams, the wall posts and the lower braces have sunk OVOLO CHAMFERS, that on the braces being carried across the centre of the tie-beam as a planted moulding. The wall trusses, the eastern with an additional moulding on the exposed face, the western unmoulded, spring from carved FOLIATED corbels. The remaining corbels are plain quadrant and fillet in form.

East block

The double doors beneath the viewing gallery lead into a small stable that temporarily housed the two or three horses awaiting their turn in the Riding School; the main stables were in the Outer Court. Two wide doorways, each formerly provided with double doors, entirely fill the north wall. The present mangers and stable divisions on the south wall are later than the original but the ghosts of the earlier division posts may be seen on the walls. The ceiling is plastered and divided by an original moulded beam.

In the northeast angle a door leads to the harness room, a square chamber with a two-light square-headed window with slightly splayed REVEALS in the centre of the north wall and a similar window, later cut through to form a doorway and finally reconverted into a window, at the east end of the south wall. The east wall is occupied by two deep segmentally headed fireplace openings by the side of which is a short passage on to the staircase. On the stair side this door, like all those in this block, has ashlar dressings with a plain sunk architrave.

The staircase, which is of wood and rises to the attic level, is arranged in straight flights with half-landings. The flights are separated by a plaster partition between NEWELS with sunk panels on the exposed faces. At the foot of the stair there is a window in the north wall and a door leading out to the Great Court. There is a two-light window in the south wall at half-landing level.

On the first floor there are two rooms, first an ante-room with a single window to north and south, plain plastered walls, a ceiling with two exposed beams and, in the west wall, a stone fireplace with a simple classic surround. Also in this wall is the door to the second room, the spectators' gallery from which distinguished visitors could watch the display below. From this side the three openings to the Riding School are treated plainly, all enclosed in a wide recess beneath a segmental arch with two plain piers projecting between the openings whose sills, some 3ft (1m) above floor level, form a balustrade. In contrast to this restrained treatment is the elaboration of the plaster cornice with its stylised DENTILS and STRAPWORK frieze in two places. The fireplace in the east wall has a more elaborate architrave moulding than that in the ante-room.

Above are two attics, each lit by a dormer on the north side similar in detail to those in the Riding School. Both rooms have fireplaces and in that in the eastern are traces of the fixings for a POT CRANE. The rooms may have served as the Riding Master's or Chief Groom's lodging.

West block

This is entered from the courtyard through a doorway similar to that of the Riding School. The doors themselves are new. It could also be reached from the Riding School through a doorway at its western end similar to that below the spectators' gallery. The two panelled doors may well be among those that replaced the doors removed under the Parliamentary Order of 1649.

Himself a proscribed delinquent and his estates in the hands of the Parliament, Newcastle wandered from Hamburg to Rotterdam, to Antwerp, Mechelen, Brussels, Valenciennes, Cambrai, Peronne and finally to Paris in April 1645, where he met and married his second wife, Margaret Lucas. Living on credit, they established themselves first in Paris and then, following Prince Charles, in Rotterdam and The Hague, where he left the prince's immediate service and retired to Antwerp.

The earl had started to acquire horses in Paris for the practice of his hobby and, in spite of continuous money troubles, gradually increased his stable and his fame among cognoscenti of the art of *manège* (horsemanship and the training of horses). In Antwerp, again on credit, he had taken over the house of Rubens the painter from his widow, and purchased his 'museum' for £1000.

Although living — as his wife records with more truth than wit — 'freely and nobly,' Newcastle was in urgent need of money and so sent Lady Newcastle and his brother, Sir Charles Cavendish, to England to negotiate for the compounding of his Derbyshire estates. The affair did not go smoothly, for not only did Parliament refuse to acknowledge Lady Newcastle as her husband's representative, on the grounds that she had married him after sequestration, but there were inevitable difficulties in raising the money. Because of delays before Parliament agreed upon a sum for which Sir Charles could compound for the estates, Bolsover had been sold to a certain Robert Thorpe for the value of its materials by the time a settlement was reached. Yet more money had to be raised to repurchase the Bolsover and Welbeck properties and to provide the subsidies so badly needed by Newcastle himself in Antwerp. After a year spent in these negotiations Sir Charles and Lady Newcastle decided to return to Holland, but Sir Charles died after a short illness without leaving England.

Lack of money did not seem to deter the earl from living in some state in Antwerp, much visited by the court and nobility, who pressed him to exhibit his horses and demonstrate his skill at *manège*. It was, indeed, at this time that he published his book on the art, illustrated with engravings which featured views of Bolsover and Welbeck. The management of his home estates he left in the hands of his two sons Henry and Charles Cavendish to whom he wrote giving instructions on the disposal of pictures and furniture from the two houses and, it seems, such repairs as would keep them habitable until his return.

Shortly before Charles II returned to England to assume the throne the earl joined the royal party at The Hague leaving, with a curious conception of gallantry, his wife in Antwerp as a security for the debts he had incurred there. In May 1660 Newcastle's exile ended with his return to London where he was joined first by his son Henry, now Earl of Ogle, and later, his wife. For a while he remained at court in attendance upon the King before obtaining permission to return to the north to see to the affairs of his Derbyshire estate which, under a private bill given the Royal Assent on 13 September 1660, were, 'restored to the Marquis of Newcastle [with] all his honours, manors, lands and tenements whereof he was in possession on the 10th day of May 1644.'

Newcastle's losses as a result of the Civil War had been vast and were calculated to be over £940 000 without accounting for the cost of repairing his damaged houses. In her *Memoirs of the Duke of Newcastle* the duchess states that he found his houses at 'Welbeck and Bolsover much out of repair ... no furniture or any necessary goods were left in them.' There is no more detailed record than this of the damage done at Bolsover while its owner was abroad. The order made by the Council of State in 1649 was specifically confined to making the buildings untenable as a castle without prejudice to their use as a private habitation and was limited to the removal of strong doors and the destruction of the outer court.

During the short period following the sale of the castle by the Committee of Derbyshire, before Sir Charles Cavendish was able to repurchase on behalf of his brother, it would seem that some pulling down had started not only in the outer court but on the main buildings as well, the lead from the gallery roof being the principal casualty. From correspondence between Newcastle and his secretary, John Rolleston, some incomplete details may be gleaned of the repairs that were necessary, for which Joseph Jackson, a mason of Bolsover, was the contractor under Andrew Clayton, the agent.

Work started in 1661 in a small way and continued at least until 1666. The slow rate of progress reflects the condition into which the estate had fallen. As late as 1665, the year in which Newcastle was created a duke by Charles II, the gallery roof was still uncovered. Andrew Clayton, reporting to the duke, wrote that the roof was ready, but that he was unable to buy the lead until such time as further rents came in.

Most of the damage appears to have been in the Terrace Range and in the private rooms in the southwest corner of the Great Court. New doors were necessary between the dining room and hall and between the gallery and hall as well as a number of others. Over the door to the Great Court the ACHIEVEMENT of arms was altered to suit Newcastle's new dignity as a duke. Windows and chimney stacks were repaired and the bridge connecting the northern end of the Terrace Range with the Fountain Garden wall walk was rebuilt,

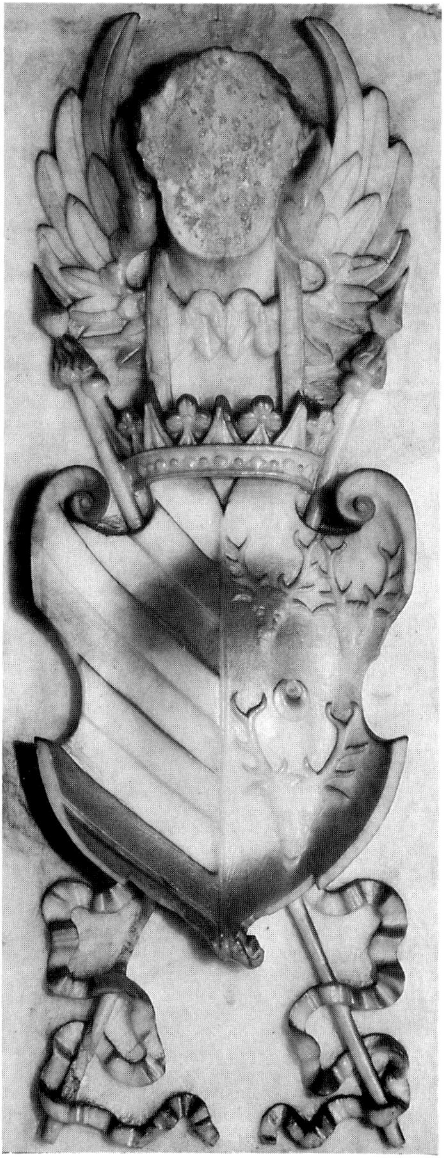

The arms of Cavendish impaling Talbot

as were the steps before the gallery door on to the terrace. It is uncertain when all this was completed but an inventory of 1670 showed the castle as being again furnished with items such as crimson taffeta and tapestry hangings and cloth-of-silver chairs.

William Cavendish, first Duke of Newcastle, who had been building and rebuilding Bolsover Castle for some fifty years since he succeeded in 1617, enjoyed it for only six or seven years after its completion. He died on Christmas Day 1676. The 'Horsemanship' duke was succeeded by his son Henry, second Duke of Newcastle, probably the last to make any regular use of the buildings. W F Goulding, in his *Bolsover Castle*, records that the second Duke, shortly before his death, commissioned a large picture of Bolsover, latterly at Welbeck, to be hung in the castle. There are no structural remains which may be attributed to the second duke, at whose death in 1691 the title became extinct and the castle passed to his heiress, Lady Margaret Cavendish. Lady Margaret married John Holles, fourth Earl of Clare, later to be Duke of Newcastle in a second creation.

The castle was evidently kept furnished by the new duke and duchess for, about 1710, it was visited by Francis, or Richard, Bassano, a heraldic painter, who made brief notes on the principal rooms and their pictures. The duchess survived her husband and until her death in 1716 Bolsover remained furnished and usable, but again there was no male heir and the castle passed to her daughter, Lady Henrietta Cavendish Holles, Countess of Oxford, who had married Edward Harley, Earl of Oxford.

Welbeck Abbey then quite supplanted Bolsover as the principal residence and during the 1740s much of the furniture and pictures were moved there and even some unspecified building was demolished to provide the stone that was taken from Bolsover to Welbeck in 1742. The final blow was not until 1751, when a new wing, the Oxford wing, was added to Welbeck and once again the Terrace Range at Bolsover was stripped to provide lead for the work. It was the Countess of Oxford who founded the school the buildings of which now occupy part of the former outer court of the castle, though the present school dates mostly from rebuildings of 1868 and 1894. One other encroachment into the outer court may be noted here: the gatehouse of 1840, in its time schoolmaster's house and vicarage, which may owe its name to its being on the site of a former gate to the outer court. Nothing, however, remains above ground to substantiate a medieval origin.

Although the Countess of Oxford stripped the Terrace Range of its roof and its furniture and added its pictures to the collection of family portraits that she was amassing at Welbeck, an inventory of her furniture, taken in 1754, the year before her death, suggest that she continued to use the Little Castle as a refuge wherein she could take tea away from the perpetual noise of the works at Welbeck. The Pillar Chamber and dining room remained furnished, the former with a great table round the central column which survived when all else had been removed, and there was her 'Tea Aequipage with a Dutch tea kettle and lamp.'

In 1755, for the third time in succession, Bolsover descended by the female line to Lady Margaret Cavendish Harley and thence at her marriage to the second Duke of Portland, in whose family it remained until 1945 when the castle was transferred by the seventh duke to the nation.

By the beginning of the nineteenth century Bolsover had fallen from being a great house to being the house of a not over-respectable suspended vicar of Bolsover, the Reverend W C Tinsley, who, with his wife, occupied two rooms of the Little Castle. Matters improved when the Reverend Hamilton Grey was appointed curate-in-charge in 1829 and paid the vicar £25 to vacate the castle so that he might improve it for his own use. Grey was impressed with the possibilities of the building but did not settle in until 1834 when he 'seriously set to work to convert the old, windy rambling, desolate looking Norman castle into a habitation fit for civilised man.'

A porch that was built on at this time on the south side has since been removed but other alterations of 1834–35 remain. The double glazing and sash windows in the Pillar Chamber and many alterations to the panelling must date from this time as well as the doorways cut between the Ante-room and Pillar Chamber and, on the floor above, from the Elysium room to the stair lobby. Hamilton Grey died in 1866 and his widow continued to occupy the Little Castle until 1883. The castle was never occupied again as a home, though in 1897, following a serious fire at the parish church, the Riding School was pressed into service as a temporary place of worship.

DESIGN OF BOLSOVER

Smithson drawings and Deipenbeke prints

The greater part of the design of the Cavendish buildings at Bolsover was carried out by three generations of the Smithson family: Robert (d1614), his son John (d1634) and grandson Huntingdon (d1648). They were a family of surveyors who continued to practise in this field for at least two further generations.

Little biographical detail of the family survives and our knowledge of them derives principally from their work and the chance survival of a volume of drawings and designs attributed to Robert and John. The collection was first mentioned by Vertue in his 1725 notebook, when the drawings were in the possession of Lord Byron, 'who got them from the family who lived at Bolsover.' They were sold in 1778 by the fifth Lord Byron to the Reverend D'Ewes Coke. His descendant Colonel W L Coke lent them to the Royal Institute of British Architects to be exhibited in 1907 when, for the first time, they attracted the attention of architectural historians. They were exhibited again in 1932, subsequently lent to and later accepted as a gift by the Royal Institute, in whose care they remain.

The drawings, known as the Smithson Collection, consist mostly of surveys of existing buildings by Robert and John Smithson. A number of original designs among them show that both were architects in the modern sense. Robert Smithson's principal work was the building of Wollaton Hall (1580–88) near Nottingham for Sir Francis Willoughby; he also designed the Countess of Shrewsbury's tomb in Derby Cathedral, erected in 1601, seven years before she died. In addition to Bolsover he worked at Longleat, Hardwick and Burton Agnes and produced designs for buildings at Welbeck Abbey and Slingsby for Sir Charles Cavendish, and at Worksop Manor for Sir Gilbert Talbot, Sir Charles's brother-in-law. When he died in 1614 the work at Welbeck, Hardwick, Slingsby and Bolsover was unfinished and all four were taken over by his son.

Most of the surviving drawings that can be attributed to Robert Smithson are surveys of existing buildings, many made in and around London, which he visited in 1609. Whether they are commissioned surveys or studies done for his own interest can only be a matter for conjecture.

John Smithson's career must have been somewhat similar. He too has left a number of unexecuted designs in addition to those for work that was actually carried out, mostly for the Cavendish family. He repeated his father's visit to London in 1618–19 but this time to considerably greater effect. The younger man found himself sent to the capital at a time when the influence of Inigo Jones and the 'artisan mannerists' was having its revolutionary effect on architectural design. That he was fired with enthusiasm for the new ideas is clear from the drawings he made, which included a gateway at Arundel House in London designed by Jones. Such was the impression that these buildings made upon him that he persuaded Sir William Cavendish to alter some of his father's partially completed work at Bolsover to conform to the new mode.

At all three Cavendish buildings the results of the London visit were clearly felt: in the scrolled and PEDIMENTED gables of the Terrace Range at Bolsover and the riding school at Welbeck; in the Bolsover gallery window design and in such details

Design by John Smithson for the doorway to the Terrace

as the southwest gateway which uses the fragment of a broken pediment over a DORIC column directly derived from the Arundel House model. Both the executed buildings and the drawings reveal that Smithson was not capable of digesting fully Inigo Jones's severe PALLADIANISM — the result was more robust than academic.

John Smithson died in 1634 and his work was continued in turn by his son, Huntingdon Smithson. None of the drawings in the collection can be attributed to Huntingdon nor do any other known buildings of his survive. There is only the epitaph on his tomb in Bolsover Church:

> Reader, beneath this plain stone buried ly
> Smithson's remainders of mortality
> Whose skill in architecture did deserve
> A fairer tomb his mem'ry to preserve

Bolsover drawings in the Smithson Collection

There are fourteen Smithson drawings of Bolsover, an unusual number to find related to one building at so early a date. None is signed but their relation to the building and their draughtsmanship show them to be the work of Robert and John. Most are working drawings intended for the craftsmen working on the building or to explain the designer's intentions to his client. Three, at least, are by Robert — a dimensioned basement plan of the Little Castle, probably the only survivor of a series of floor plans, an elevation of the hall fireplace and a perspective sketch for what later became the Elysium Room. This last design, which was eventually adapted for use in the Marble Closet by John Smithson, shows the side walls covered by hangings suspended from poles. Three more drawings relate to the Little Castle, the kitchen fireplace, the steps to the porch and the niches on the staircase, and may be Robert's designs though executed by his son.

The remaining Bolsover drawings are all by John Smithson and clearly show the influence of his London visit of 1618. They include details of the doors to the wall walk from the Little Castle and, in the Terrace Range, the hall entry door and the great gallery doorcase with the balcony over it. None but the last varies from the building as executed and this only in detail.

There are two variants on the fountain design and details of the pool and central pedestal. Perhaps the most significant is the dimensioned plan showing his 1617–20 proposal for completing the Terrage Range after the 1617 pause. It includes that part of the range south of the apartments which had been almost completed before Sir Charles's death and may be one of the set of plans used by the painter Deipenbeke for his view of the Terrace.

The proposal was for a double range with two storeys towards the court and a single-storey gallery and ante-rooms along the Terrace. At the north end, facing the court, was to be the great hall, which must already have formed part of Robert Smithson's plans, separated from the apartments by a grand staircase. Another stair was planned to the south which served the state rooms and the private apartments. Projecting from the southern end of the range was a curious chapel, circular in plan, labelled on the drawing 'The Steeple.' This plan was never fully carried out. When work was suspended the hall, gallery and grand stair were complete but the two-storey state apartments were never built.

Deipenbeke prints

In 1658 William Cavendish, Marquess of Newcastle, while still in exile, published in Antwerp his treatise on horsemanship. The book, entitled '*La Méthode et Invention Nouvelle de Dresser les Chevaux* ...' was illustrated by engravings of the author demonstrating various forms of dressage. They were executed by a variety of engravers from paintings by Abraham Deipenbeke [born at Bois-le-Duc ('s Hertogenbosch), a former pupil of Rubens, director of the Academy of Antwerp from 1641 and died in 1675]. They show in their backgrounds views of Welbeck Abbey and Bolsover Castle, Sir William's principal houses. Apart from their intrinsic interest, the engravings are of considerable value as contemporary illustrations of the two houses.

Although the marquess did not publish his book until 1658, material for the background for the illustrations had been gathered considerably earlier. Their treatment of Bolsover shows that they were not drawn on the spot but from sketches made about 1620, either by the artist himself or from lost architectural drawings similar to those surviving in the Smithson Collection. Even making allowance for the

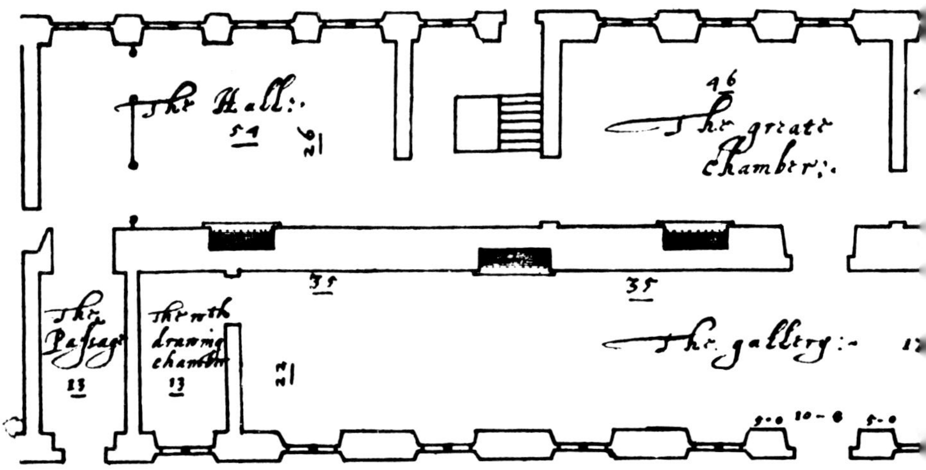

Plan by John Smithson, c1617–20, showing his proposal for completing the Terrace Range

fact that the foregrounds are all formal compositions introduced by the artist to frame the pictures and not related to the building, they represent the castle in a state which could not, in fact, ever have existed. On the other hand their treatment is sufficiently accurate to suggest that those details that were completed at the time are correctly delineated.

That showing the Terrace façade throws interesting light on the development of the design. The omission of the Terrace may be discounted as being artist's licence. The gallery is shown with its projecting PILASTERS complete but must have been drawn from a proposal and not from the actual building. The pediments to the gallery windows are shown alike, whereas in execution they were alternated and the stairs to the central door are omitted. Even more significant, the feature above this door is shown to correspond to a drawing for it by John Smithson which varies in detail from the design as executed. Beyond the gallery, Robert Smithson's gables are shown unaltered as they were before his son conceived the device of continuing his gallery parapet and adding further pilasters to unify the Terrace façade. Not only does this enable the success of John Smithson's device to be appreciated but it shows him to be a designer capable of seizing an opportunity and turning it to his advantage.

Other variations confirm that the paintings were a pastiche of proposal and executed design. The details of the forecourt to the Little Castle vary among the engravings. This is understandable as the pavilions and enclosing wall would have

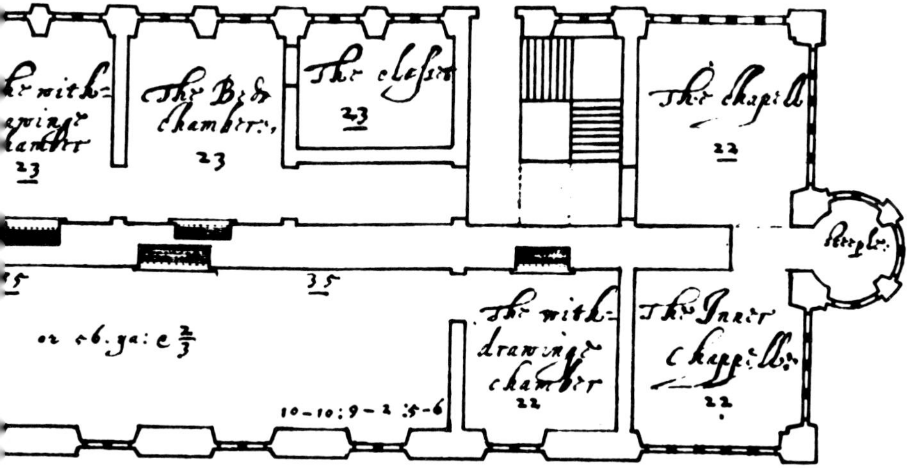

been only partly finished at the time; similarly the gateway from the Great Court to the Fountain Garden is shown before Huntingdon Smithson altered it to lie on the axis of his Riding School. It is significant too that the boundary wall of the Great Court, not built until 1634, is missing and that the Venus Fountain, the design for which had not been settled by 1620, is shown incorrectly.

APPENDIX

Sequence of building

Dr Mark Girouard has proposed an alternative sequence of building to that described in this handbook. Details are given in his book, *Robert Smythson and the Elizabethan County House* (second edition) 1983.

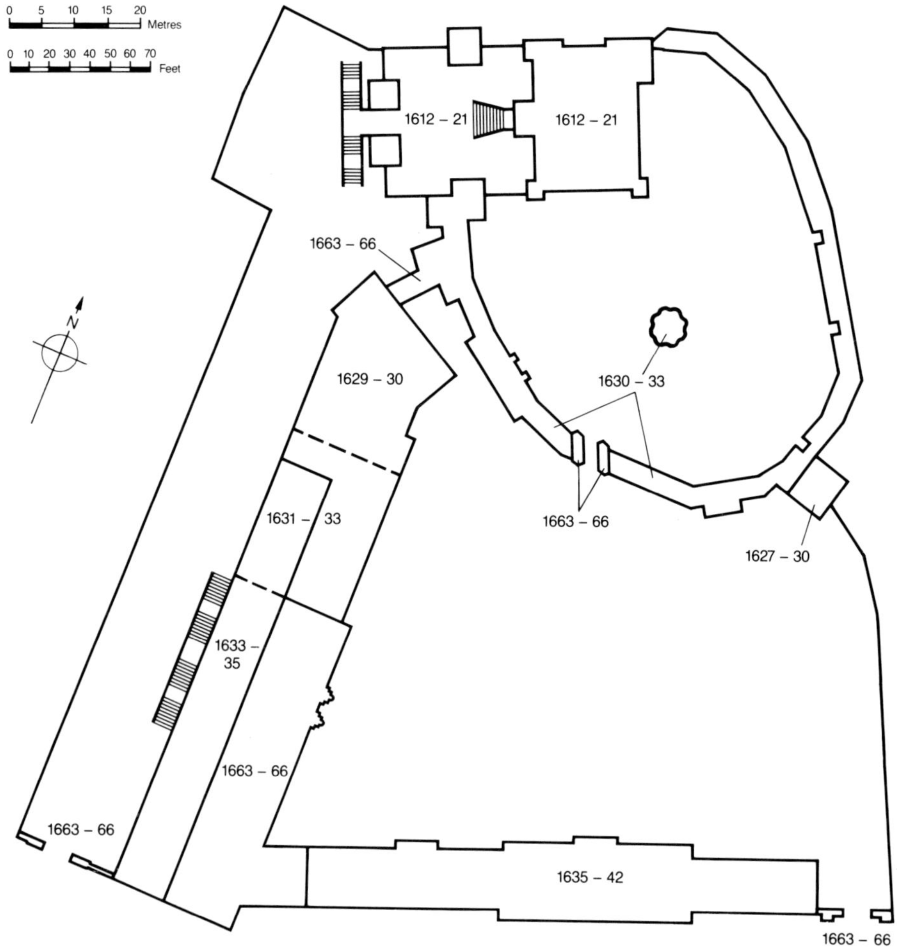

Mark Girouard's dating scheme

1612 – 21	Sir Charles & Sir William Cavendish	Robert/John Smithson
1627 – 30	Sir William Cavendish	John Smithson
1630 – 35	Sir William Cavendish	John/Huntingdon Smithson
1635 – 40	Sir William Cavendish	Huntingdon Smithson
1663 – 66	Duke of Newcastle	Samuel Marsh

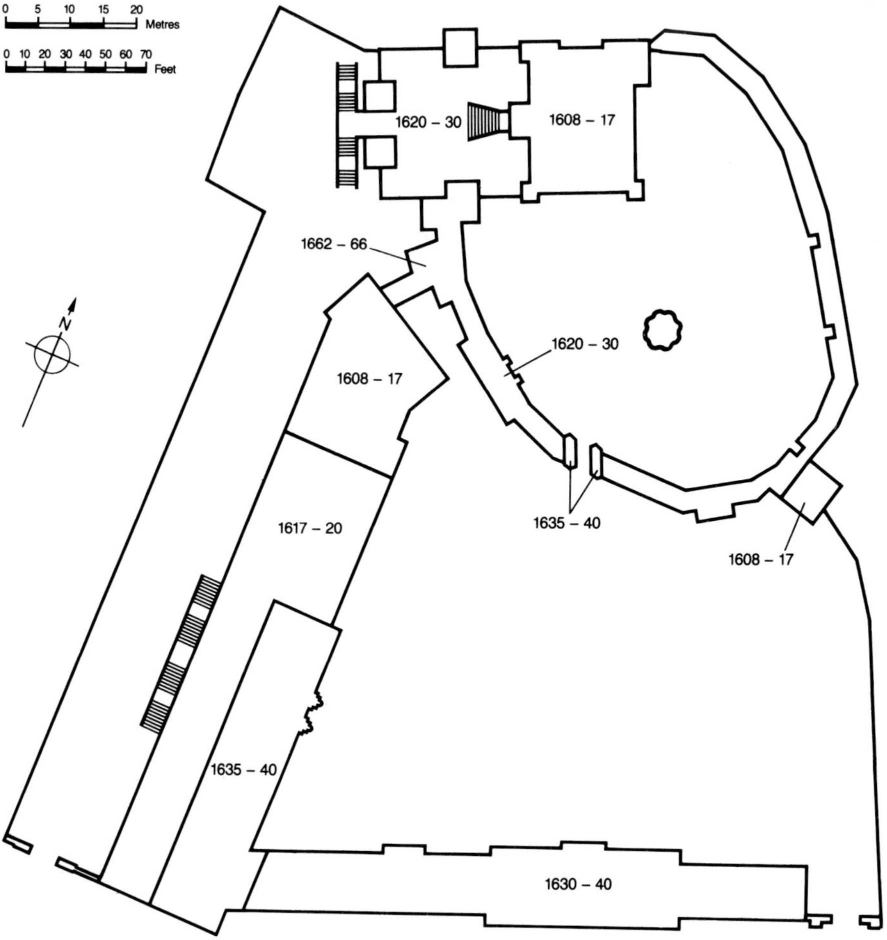

Patrick Faulkner's dating scheme

1608 – 17	Sir Charles Cavendish	Robert/John Smithson
1617 – 20	Sir William Cavendish	John Smithson
1620 – 30	Sir William Cavendish	John Smithson
1630 – 34	Sir William Cavendish	Huntingdon Smithson
1635 – 40	Sir William Cavendish	Anon
1662 – 66	Duke of Newcastle	Anon

GLOSSARY

Abacus (Abaci) Flat slab immediately above the capital of a column
Achievement Armorial shield displayed with its complete accessories: helm, crest, supporters, etc.
Aedicule Framing of a window or door by columns an entablature and pediment
Arabesque Surface ornament consisting of flowing stem and leaf forms wildly intertwined
Architrave Lowest division of the emblature; also, the ornamental band round a door or corridor opeing
Ashlar Squared stone laid in regular courses with fine joints
Bailey Walled enclosure or courtyard in a castle
Ball finial See Finial
Baluster Short pillar supporting a handrail or coping
Balustrade Series of balusters and coping
Baroque Exuberant style using elements of classical architecture
Barrel vault Continuous arched vault of semicircular section
Battlement Parapet with openings (embrasures) between raised portions (merlons)

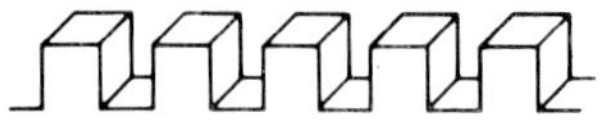

Crenellation (battlements)

Bolection Moulding around a panel, projecting beyond the surface of the framing
Boss Ornamental projection concealing the intersection of the ribs or beams of a vault or ceiling
Capital Ornamental head of a column or pillar
Caryatid Female figure used instead of a column to support an entablature
Chamfer Bevelled edge
Composite Blend of two orders of architecture (see Order)
Console Scroll-like bracket
Coping Protective stone capping to a wall; sloping and projecting to shed water
Corbel Projection from a wall to support a beam or other weight

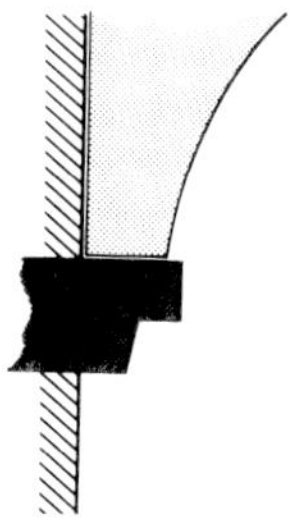

Corbel

Corinthian See Order
Cornice Projection near the top of a wall; ornamental moulding round a room where walls and ceiling meet
Crenellation Battlement
Cresting Ornamental finish along the top of a screen, etc
Cupola Small turret capped with a dome; or the dome itself
Curtain wall Wall enclosing a courtyard
Dado Lower part of a room or wall when lined or painted separately from the rest
Dentil One of a series of square blocks or projections
Die Supporting block or solid portion of balustrade
Doric See Order

Entablature Uppermost part of a classical order (q.v.). It consists of three parts: the upper projecting cornice; the frieze, which when it swells outwards is said to be pulvinated; and the lower member, the architrave.

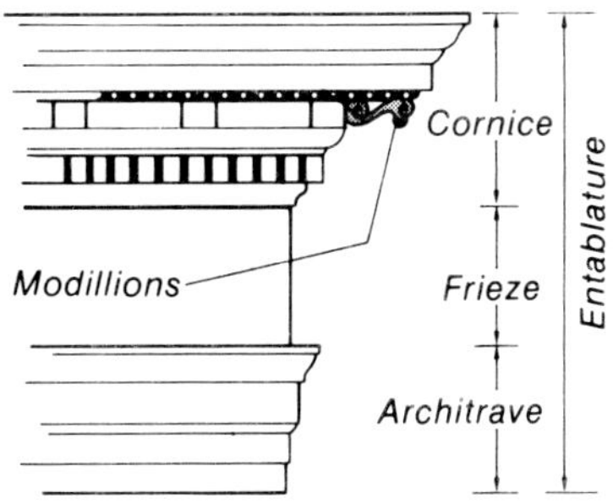

Entablature

Fenestration Arrangement of windows
Fielded panel Panel with raised central area
Fillet Narrow flat raised band
Finial Ornament at the top of a spire, gable, etc
Foliated Covered with leaf ornament
Frieze In classical architecture, horizontal band of decoration, immediately below the cornice
Groin Edge formed by the intersection of two vaults
Honour Large feudal estate, usually centred on a castle
Impale Heraldically, to marshal side by side two coats of arms on a single shield
Impost Brackets in walls on which the ends of an arch rest
Ionic See Order
Jewelled Decorated with projecting jewel-shaped insets, often in vari-coloured marble or plaster
Keep Great tower, usually used of eleventh- or twelfth-century buildings, but sometimes loosely of those of later date
King post Vertical post extending from a tie beam to the apex of a roof
Kneeler Block of stone set at the base of an eave's coping
Label mould Projecing weather moulding above a window or door; hood mould
Lintel Horizontal beam or stone over a doorway, window or fireplace
Loop Narrow opening for the discharge of arrows or to admit light; cross loop, in the form of a cross
Lunette Semicircular or crescent shaped space where a vault intersects a wall or other vault
Masons' lodge Workshop used by a group of masons
Mullion, Transom Vertical and horizontal members dividing a window
Newel Central post or column around which winds a spiral staircase
Ogee Double curve (S or reversed-S profile)
Order Name applied to the system of base, column, capital and entablature, based on antique Greek or Roman models. There are four principal models whose details tend to follow a fixed pattern: Doric, Ionic, Composite, Corinthian
Ovolo Moulding forming a quarter round in section
Palladian In the architectural style introduced by Andrea Palladio in the sixteenth century
Parapet Low protective wall at the edge of a roof
Parterre A flower garden with beds arranged in a regular geometric pattern
Pediment A gable-like form used above an entablature in classical architecture. Such a device used to cap a door or window. The top may be triangular or curved as a segment of a circle (segmental); it may be interrupted at the centre (broken)
Pilaster Shallow projecting column on a wall, usually with rectangular cross-section
Plinth Projecting masonry at the base of a wall

Pot crane Swinging iron bracket used to support a cooking vessel over a fire

Principal Large rafter forming part of a truss

Pulvinated See Entablature

Purlin Longitudinal horizontal beam linking principal rafters and supporting common rafters

Putti Small naked boys in Renaissance sculpture

Queen posts Pair of vertical posts standing on the tie beam and supporting the side purlins or principals

Quoins Squared stones used to finish the corner of a building

Reveal Vertical sides of window or door opening

Rustication Stonework with projecting roughened areas

Screens passage Cross passage with entrances to kitchen, buttery and pantry, separated from a medieval great hall by wooden partitions or screens

Scrollwork Decorative device simulating paper with rolled edges.

Soffit Under surface of an arch, lintel, canopy, etc

Spandrel Triangular space above the curved sides of an arch

Splay Side of a window by which the opening widens towards the inner face of the wall

Springing Intersection at each side of an arch between its lower surface and the faces of the walls or piers carrying it

Staff bead Roll or staff running along the angle of an opening

Stillage Raised bench on which wine or beer casks are stored

Strapwork Decoration with the character of studded weather bands

String-course Projecting horizontal band of masonry across the front of, or around all the walls of, a building

Touch Black Derbyshire marble

Tracery Decorative work formed by the ornamental intersection of the mullions in the upper part of a window

Transom See Mullion

Truss Pair of rafters joined with others to make a rigid frame to support a roof

Vermiculation Worm-like decoration covering a surface

Voussoir Wedge-like stone forming one of the pieces of an arch